ANDY MURRAY BIOGRAPHY

The Rise of a Tennis Legend From Dunblane to Centre Court

Jody E. Parks

Copyright @ 2024 by Jody E. Parks

All rights reserved. No part of this book may be reproduced, distributed, or transmitted in any form or by any means, including photocopying, recording, or other electronic or mechanical methods, without the prior written permission of the publisher, except in the case of brief quotations embodied in critical reviews and specific other noncommercial uses permitted by copyright law.

This book is a work of nonfiction. Names, characters, places, and incidents either are products of the author's imagination or are used fictitiously. Any resemblance to actual events or locales or persons, living or dead, is entirely coincidental.

Disclaimer

The following book is for entertainment and informational purposes only. The information presented is without contract or any type of guarantee assurance. While every caution has been taken to provide accurate and current information, it is solely the reader's responsibility to check all information contained in this article before relying upon it. Neither the author nor the publisher can be held accountable for any errors or omissions. Under no circumstances will any legal responsibility or blame be held against the author or publisher for any reparation, damages, or monetary loss due to the information presented, either directly or indirectly. This book is not intended as legal or medical advice. If any such specialized advice is needed, seek a qualified individual for help.

Trademarks are used without permission. Use of the trademark is not authorized by, associated with, or sponsored by the trademark owners. All trademarks and brands used within this book are used with no intent to infringe on the trademark owners and are only used for clarifying purposes.

This book is not sponsored by or affiliated with Tennis, its teams, the players, or anyone involved with them.

Table of Content

INTRODUCTION.. 5

CHAPTER 1: EARLY LIFE AND
BEGINNINGS.. 11

CHAPTER 2: JUNIOR CAREER..................... 17

CHAPTER 3: PROFESSIONAL DEBUT.........23

CHAPTER 4: RISE TO PROMINENCE..........30

CHAPTER 5: FIRST GRAND SLAM SUCCESS
37

CHAPTER 6: OLYMPIC GLORY.................... 48

CHAPTER 7: INJURIES AND COMEBACKS...
61

CHAPTER 8: SECOND GRAND SLAM WIN 75

CHAPTER 9: WORLD NO. 1............................ 83

CHAPTER 10: LATER CAREER AND
LEGACY.. 90

CONCLUSION.. 97

INTRODUCTION

One of the finest sportsmen in British history, Andy Murray is known for his perseverance, tenacity, and intense competitive spirit on the tennis field. Andrew Barron Murray was born in Glasgow, Scotland, on May 15, 1987. Encouraged by a family that was ardently involved in tennis, Murray showed potential in the game from an early age. Andy's brother Jamie, who would also become a great doubles player, and mother Judy Murray, who was a tennis instructor herself, developed Andy's skills.

Murray showed unrelenting attention and devotion to his art from a young age. His ascent through the junior tennis levels was quick, and his triumphs gave rise to expectations of future greatness. Murray was well-known for his strong groundstrokes, tactical sense, and capacity to outlast opponents in demanding matches by the time he went professional in 2005.

Murray's path has been characterized by perseverance in the face of difficulty throughout his career. He has persevered despite failures and injuries, showing an amazing capacity to get better every time. One of the pinnacles of his career occurred in 2012 when he won his maiden Grand Slam title at the US Open, making history as the first British male to win a major singles trophy in 76 years. In addition to securing his status as one of the game's best players, this triumph gave British tennis fans newfound optimism and a sense of pride in their country.

But Murray would make his mark in the annals of sports mythology on the immaculate Wimbledon grass courts. His victory in the Wimbledon men's singles tournament in 2013 put an end to Britain's 77-year drought, a momentous occasion that sent shockwaves across the sports globe. Murray's victory was a tribute to his unshakable will and the years of arduous practice he had put into perfecting his skill.

Murray's influence goes much beyond his achievements on the tennis court. His charitable endeavors, which include backing cancer research and promoting gender parity in athletics, demonstrate a strong desire to change the world for the better. Murray is respected not just as a champion athlete but also as a role model and an ambassador for the sport because of his humility and grounded personality, which has won him over followers all over the world.

Fans and aspiring sportsmen alike find inspiration in Andy Murray's career as he pursues tennis greatness. The actual definition of a sporting hero is embodied by his unshakable dedication, tenacity in the face of adversity, and devotion to making a meaningful difference both on and off the field. Whether he was fighting for his life on the tennis court or supporting causes near and dear to his heart, Andy Murray left an enduring impression on the world of sports and beyond.

His professional life is proof of the transformational potential of tenacity and fortitude. A succession of highs and lows along the way have molded Murray into the champion and role model he is today, despite the trophies and accolades. In addition to defining his career, his capacity to rise above misfortune has won him admirers worldwide.

Murray's rise to the top of men's tennis continued in 2013 as he achieved another significant victory at Wimbledon, after his breakthrough at the US Open in 2012. In addition to putting an end to Britain's lengthy wait for a male singles winner, the triumph on the All England Club's hallowed lawns solidified Murray's reputation as a national hero. His emotional victory and the resolute backing of the British audience demonstrated his steely will and resilience under duress.

Murray's career took off in the years that followed as he persistently upended the supremacy of tennis greats like Rafael Nadal, Roger Federer, and Novak Djokovic. In particular, Murray's rivalry with Djokovic led to incredible on-court skirmishes that showcased his tactical skill and capacity to modify his style of play to counteract his opponents' advantages.

Murray's trip has not, however, been without difficulties. Several times, injuries, especially to his hip, have put his willpower to the test and almost ended his career. Murray was on the verge of retiring due to the physical toll of playing professional tennis as well as the demands of intense training and competition. But as always, he refused to let hardship get to him and had many operations as well as rigorous rehabilitation to get back to his best.

Murray's remarkable recovery tale is evidence of both his unyielding will and his team's and his supporters' unfailing support. His comeback to competitive tennis, characterized by spirited wins and moving examples of fortitude, has motivated other people to overcome similar obstacles.

His support of several humanitarian issues has an influence that goes beyond tennis. He has advocated for equal pay and opportunity for female athletes and has been a prominent supporter of women's rights in sports. Fans and other athletes alike appreciate and admire him for his efforts to advance diversity and inclusiveness in the sport.

The history of tennis will always be forever altered by Murray's legacy as a champion, ally, and role model, even as he writes the next chapter of his remarkable career. The enormous influence of his journey is shown by his ability to inspire generations of players and transcend the sport. Andy Murray's persistent dedication to greatness and tenacity, whether he is contending for Grand Slam titles or supporting social issues, continues to inspire adoration and respect globally.

CHAPTER 1: EARLY LIFE AND BEGINNINGS

One of the finest sportsmen in British history, Andy Murray is known for his perseverance, tenacity, and intense competitive spirit on the tennis field. Andrew Barron Murray was born in Glasgow, Scotland, on May 15, 1987. Encouraged by a family that was ardently involved in tennis, Murray showed potential in the game from an early age. Andy's brother Jamie, who would also become a great doubles player, and mother Judy Murray, who was a tennis instructor herself, developed Andy's skills.

Murray showed unrelenting attention and devotion to his art from a young age. His ascent through the junior tennis levels was quick, and his triumphs gave rise to expectations of future greatness. Murray was well-known for his strong groundstrokes, tactical sense, and capacity to outlast opponents in demanding matches by the time he went professional in 2005.

Murray's path has been characterized by perseverance in the face of difficulty throughout his career. He has persevered despite failures and injuries, showing an amazing capacity to get better every time. One of the pinnacles of his career occurred in 2012 when he won his maiden Grand Slam title at the US Open, making history as the first British male to win a major singles trophy in 76 years. In addition to securing his status as one of the game's best players, this triumph gave British tennis fans newfound optimism and a sense of pride in their country.

But Murray would make his mark in the annals of sports mythology on the immaculate Wimbledon grass courts. His victory in the Wimbledon men's singles tournament in 2013 put an end to Britain's 77-year drought, a momentous occasion that sent shockwaves across the sports globe. Murray's victory was a tribute to his unshakable will and the years of arduous practice he had put into perfecting his skill.

Murray's influence goes much beyond his achievements on the tennis court. His charitable endeavors, which include backing cancer research and promoting gender parity in athletics, demonstrate a strong desire to change the world for the better. Murray is respected not just as a champion athlete but also as a role model and an ambassador for the sport because of his humility and grounded personality, which has won him over followers all over the world.

Fans and aspiring sportsmen alike find inspiration in Andy Murray's career as he pursues tennis greatness. The actual definition of a sporting hero is embodied by his unshakable dedication, tenacity in the face of adversity, and devotion to making a meaningful difference both on and off the field. Whether he was fighting for his life on the tennis court or supporting causes near and dear to his heart, Andy Murray left an enduring impression on the world of sports and beyond.

His professional life is proof of the transformational potential of tenacity and fortitude. A succession of highs and lows along the way have molded Murray into the champion and role model he is today, despite the trophies and accolades. In addition to defining his career, his capacity to rise above misfortune has won him admirers worldwide.

Murray's rise to the top of men's tennis continued in 2013 as he achieved another significant victory at Wimbledon, after his breakthrough at the US Open in 2012. In addition to putting an end to Britain's lengthy wait for a male singles winner, the triumph on the All England Club's hallowed lawns solidified Murray's reputation as a national hero. His emotional victory and the resolute backing of the British audience demonstrated his steely will and resilience under duress.

Murray's career took off in the years that followed as he persistently upended the supremacy of tennis greats like Rafael Nadal, Roger Federer, and Novak Djokovic. In particular, Murray's rivalry with Djokovic led to incredible on-court skirmishes that showcased his tactical skill and capacity to modify his style of play to counteract his opponents' advantages.

Murray's trip has not, however, been without difficulties. Several times, injuries, especially to his hip, have put his willpower to the test and almost ended his career. Murray was on the verge of retiring due to the physical toll of playing professional tennis as well as the demands of intense training and competition. But as always, he refused to let hardship get to him and had many operations as well as rigorous rehabilitation to get back to his best.

Murray's remarkable recovery tale is evidence of both his unyielding will and his team's and his supporters' unfailing support. His comeback to competitive tennis, characterized by spirited wins and moving examples of fortitude, has motivated other people to overcome similar obstacles.

His support of several humanitarian issues has an influence that goes beyond tennis. He has advocated for equal pay and opportunity for female athletes and has been a prominent supporter of women's rights in sports. Fans and other athletes alike appreciate and admire him for his efforts to advance diversity and inclusiveness in the sport.

The history of tennis will always be forever altered by Murray's legacy as a champion, ally, and role model, even as he writes the next chapter of his remarkable career. The enormous influence of his journey is shown by his ability to inspire generations of players and transcend the sport. Andy Murray's persistent dedication to greatness and tenacity, whether he is contending for Grand Slam titles or supporting social issues, continues to inspire adoration and respect globally.

CHAPTER 2: JUNIOR CAREER

Andy Murray's junior career offers evidence of his early potential and tenacity in the tennis world. Murray showed extraordinary skill and a strong sense of competition from an early age, traits that would help him succeed in the professional ranks. Murray was up in Dunblane, Scotland, and started playing tennis under the tutelage of his mother Judy, a former tennis instructor.

It was clear from the beginning that Murray had a natural talent for the game. Even as a young child, he showed a strong competitive spirit by participating in junior competitions throughout the United Kingdom and beyond. Murray gained recognition for his technical skill set almost away, especially for his strong groundstrokes and court smarts. Even among his colleagues, he was unique in his ability to read opponents and predict their next actions.

Murray's commitment to working out and raising his level of play was evident as he rose through the junior divisions. He developed his abilities under the guidance of several coaches who saw his potential and fostered his gift. Murray's rise in junior tennis was characterized by noteworthy triumphs and accomplishments, such as his first major victory in the Boys' 12 category at the esteemed Orange Bowl in 1999. Murray's early success gave him confidence that he could compete at the top levels of the sport and provided a strong platform for his future aspirations.

During his collegiate career, Murray triumphed against obstacles that put his fortitude to the test. His involvement in junior competitions honed his competitive spirit and influenced his style of play. Murray's unwavering commitment to perfection and his never-ending quest for progress helped him reach new heights and paved the way for his move to the professional circuit.

Aside from his technical prowess and passion for competition, Murray's poise and sportsmanship on the court defined his junior career. He gained recognition for his maturity beyond his years and his capacity to manage stressful conditions. These characteristics would also come to define his professional career, winning him the respect of both opponents and teammates.

Murray had solidified his status as a rising talent in the tennis world as his junior career came to an end. His successes in minor competitions offered a taste of the brilliance he would experience in his professional career. Murray's progression from a gifted young prospect to a Grand Slam winner is a testament to both his extraordinary skill and his persistent commitment to his craft.

Murray's junior career was more than simply a string of wins; it was also a developmental time when he developed the abilities and frame of mind that would make him one of the best tennis players of all time. His mother Judy Murray, who was instrumental in influencing his tennis growth, oversaw his early years on the court during rigorous training sessions that frequently lasted hours. From the beginning, Murray stood out from his contemporaries with a unique combination of mental toughness, agility, and tactical knowledge.

Junior tennis competitions taught Murray important lessons about resiliency and flexibility. He played against a wide range of opponents, each of whom offered different difficulties that compelled him to hone his skills and extend his strategic thinking. Murray's ability to assess matches and modify his strategy accordingly became a defining characteristic of his style of play and helped set the stage for his subsequent success on the ATP circuit.

Murray won a lot of big matches throughout his junior career, which highlighted his growing reputation in the tennis community. His victory over Sergiy Stakhovsky in straight sets at the 2004 US Open Junior championship demonstrated his capacity to execute well under duress on a large platform. In addition to giving Murray more self-assurance, this historic win cemented his status as a young talent with the ability to play at the top levels of professional tennis.

His junior years were marked by a dedication to physical training and an unwavering quest for progress. He spent endless hours honing his skills, strengthening his footwork, and fortifying his mental toughness—all essential elements of his competitive toolkit. Murray's natural ability and his intense training program provided a strong basis for the difficulties he would face in his professional career.

Murray's junior career was a tribute to his sportsmanship and honesty as a competitor, regardless of his accomplishments. Both supporters and teammates praised him for his poise in winning and tenacity in losing. Murray became a global celebrity and a role model for young sportsmen due to his ability to manage the highs and lows of competition with grace and humility.

Murray took the priceless knowledge and experiences from his early years with him as he made the switch from junior tennis to the professional ranks. In addition to developing his technical abilities and strategic sense, his junior career gave him a strong work ethic and a love of the game that would later characterize his incredible path to becoming an Olympic gold medalist and multiple Grand Slam winner.

His junior career is proof of the transformational potential that comes from commitment, tenacity, and self-belief. Future generations of players can draw inspiration from his path from a young, gifted player in Dunblane to a worldwide tennis star. It shows the critical role that passion and perseverance play in reaching success both on and off the court. His remarkable legacy in the tennis world is proof of the lasting impact of his younger years, which planted the seeds for his remarkable career.

CHAPTER 3: PROFESSIONAL DEBUT

Despite his youth, Andy Murray showed his determination when he entered the professional tennis scene. His debut was characterized by a raw talent that grabbed viewers and sent shockwaves across the tennis world, even though specific dates may fade from recollection. Murray, who was inspired by his unlikely rise to the top of the sport, was born in Dunblane, Scotland. His family and instructors instilled in him a strong work ethic and a fiery resolve that influenced his early years.

Murray demonstrated an early grasp of the game as a young player, combining tactical awareness with an exceptional capacity to perform well under duress. These traits came together to build a powerful skill set that would characterize his career upon his professional debut. Murray had a lasting impression on the game from the beginning, whether it was via his unwavering focus on practice and game day determination, or both.

His inaugural contests were exhibitions of mental toughness as much as athletic prowess. Murray's technique became known for his ability to modify his game to suit different opponents and situations. He used every game as a canvas to depict a story of tenacity and cunning, winning the respect and admiration of both teammates and commentators.

Although Murray would go on to win many titles and get many honors, his professional debut provided a model for what was to come. It was evidence of his steadfast self-belief and his ability to go beyond any barriers in his way. Every phase of Murray's journey, from the stressful early years of his career to the victorious celebrations that would mark his later years, was anchored in the foundation set during those early encounters.

Beyond the numbers and titles, Murray's debut marked the start of a new chapter in tennis history. He distinguished himself as a force to be reckoned with on any surface with his unique combination of power and elegance as well as his unrivaled competitive spirit. His resilience amid the intense pressure of Grand Slam competitions and the arduous schedule of the ATP Tour said volumes about his character and commitment to the game.

His professional debut was more than simply a set of games; it was the beginning of a career characterized by tenacity, willpower, and an unwavering quest for excellence. It established the foundation for a legacy that would stretch beyond the realm of sports, encouraging many young athletes to have huge dreams and put in endless hours to realize them. That first stride onto the professional tennis stage marked the beginning of his journey from a gifted young player to a tennis superstar, and it would influence the game's future for years to come.

His professional debut was a turning point in tennis history, both for him and for the sport as a whole. Murray, who was raised in Dunblane, Scotland, exhibited promise from an early age and had developed a level of concentration on the court that belied his youth. In addition to being a step up in difficulty, his ascent to the professional ranks was the result of years of selflessness, diligence, and unflinching faith in his ability.

When Murray entered the professional arena, he was met with an overwhelming number of obstacles. More than simply technical skill was needed to make the jump from junior competitions to the brutal ATP Tour stadiums; one also needed mental toughness and the capacity to handle the severe scrutiny that comes with competing at the highest level. However, Murray's debut was characterized by a furious resolve to leave his imprint rather than reluctance.

Murray's playing showed flashes of brilliance in those early encounters, flashes that would later come to characterize his style. His ability to adjust his play to take advantage of his opponent's flaws and accentuate his strengths demonstrated his tactical awareness and strategic savvy. Murray displayed maturity beyond his years, using each match as a canvas to paint a story of tenacity and inventiveness.

Murray's debut demonstrated his mental toughness in addition to his technical skill. Matches frequently hung precariously, and Murray showed an amazing capacity for composure in the face of stress. His ability to remain composed under pressure became a defining characteristic of his game, winning him the admiration of both opponents and supporters.

His debut attracted a greater degree of notice and investigation. As commentators discussed the possibilities of this young Scottish genius, media curiosity grew. But Murray never wavered from his art, fending off outside pressure with a cool exterior that belied the fire blazing inside.

Murray's desire to play at the top level was fueled by his growing confidence as victories started to pile up. From the physical rigors of exhausting bouts to the mental battles champions battled, every tournament presented fresh insights and obstacles. Murray's work ethic and desire for achievement were evident in his abilities to change and modify his style of play in reaction to these difficulties.

In retrospect, Murray's professional debut marked a turning point not just in his career but also in the development of contemporary tennis. His ascent through the ranks heralded a change in the sport, a time when physical prowess, mental tenacity, and talent came together to redefine what it meant to be a champion. Murray's transformation from a bright young player to a Grand Slam contender struck a chord with tennis fans all across the world, encouraging a new generation of athletes to aim high and achieve greatness.

In addition to the honors and prizes that would come with it, Murray's debut set the stage for a career characterized by tenacity, fortitude, and an unwavering quest for excellence. It demonstrated the strength of conviction and willpower and demonstrated that, in the realm of professional athletics, everything is achievable with a great deal of effort and commitment. His rise from tennis rookie to icon status is proof of the transformational power of sport and the long-lasting effects of passion, tenacity, and the constant pursuit of perfection.

CHAPTER 4: RISE TO PROMINENCE

Andy Murray's meteoric climb to fame in the tennis world is a credit to his extraordinary skill, steadfast work ethic, and unshakable resolve. Murray, who was raised in Dunblane, Scotland, developed a keen interest in tennis at a young age. His mother Judy Murray, a former professional player and tennis instructor, helped him improve. Murray's commitment to the game was clear from an early age; he spent endless hours honing his skills and grit on the court.

Murray made a name for himself as a junior by displaying a unique blend of quickness, agility, and tactical awareness. His breakthrough came in 2004 when he took home the junior US Open trophy, indicating a bright future for himself. Murray's climb to the top of the professional tennis ranks began the following year when he made his ATP Tour debut.

Murray's capacity to constantly change and modify his style of play has been one of his most distinctive qualities. Initially renowned for his skill in counterpunching and defense, he progressively evolved into a more aggressive player, adding strong groundstrokes and a devastating serve to his skill set. Murray's unwavering quest for perfection, which frequently involved pushing himself to the edge of his physical and mental capabilities, served as the foundation for this progression.

He made his Grand Slam debut in 2008 when he advanced to the US Open final, becoming the first British player to do so in more than ten years. Murray's performance in the match, even though he lost, announced his entrance as a contender on the world tennis scene. He kept gaining ground, winning his first Masters 1000 championship in the 2008 Cincinnati Masters and establishing himself as one of the world's top players.

But Murray cemented his place in tennis history at Wimbledon in 2012. He overcame Novak Djokovic in a thrilling final to become the first male British player to win the coveted singles championship in 77 years. The triumph solidified Murray's reputation as a national hero and a sports legend while also putting an end to Britain's protracted search for a Wimbledon winner.

Murray's ascent to the top of the global rankings in 2016 was yet another career high point and demonstrated his dependability and fortitude in the face of tough opposition. He struggled through hardships and ailments, including a hip injury that threatened to end his career, so his triumph wasn't without challenges. Despite these difficulties, Murray's willpower and endurance did not waver as he faced many surgeries and arduous rehabilitation to resume his professional tennis career.

Outside of his accomplishments on the tennis court, Murray's influence is widespread. He has been a strong supporter of equal prize money for male and female athletes and has frequently spoken out against sexism in the sports world. Notable have been his charity endeavors, which include his backing of several projects and charitable groups that provide young people with access to sports and education.

His extraordinary skill, unshakable work ethic, and unrelenting drive to achieve against all circumstances are the reasons for his climb to notoriety. Murray's path from his early years as a talented junior player to becoming the world No. 1 and multiple Grand Slam winner has inspired numerous fans worldwide and permanently altered the game of tennis.

The story of Andy Murray's rise to fame is one of tenacity, fortitude, and the unwavering quest for excellence in the fiercely competitive world of professional tennis. After winning Wimbledon for the first time in history in 2012, Murray's career trajectory appeared set to soar even higher. On the ATP Tour, he kept up his impressive play, persistently undermining the supremacy of tennis greats such as Rafael Nadal, Novak Djokovic, and Roger Federer.

Following his Wimbledon victory, he experienced several noteworthy successes and turning points in his life. Murray won his second Wimbledon championship in 2013, adding to his Grand Slam total. This achievement highlighted Murray's resilience on the biggest stage of the sport. His triumph at Wimbledon cemented his standing as a dangerous grass-court player and won him many more admirers throughout the globe.

Murray's influence went beyond personal achievements since he was instrumental in bringing British tennis back to life and instilling hope in the minds of the next players. His achievements in the 2012 London Olympics, when he won a silver medal in mixed doubles and a gold medal in singles, solidified his reputation as a national hero and symbol of sports. Fans were immensely moved by his emotional victory on home ground, which demonstrated his bravery and perseverance in the face of extreme pressure and expectations.

Despite fierce competition from his rivals, Murray's tactical skill, strategic awareness, and persistent dedication to perfection allowed him to maintain his dominance on the ATP Tour. Men's tennis gained a captivating dynamic from his competition with Djokovic, Nadal, and Federer, as each player pushed the limits of athleticism and talent to win Grand Slam titles.

His lobbying activities and charitable endeavors have left a lasting legacy. He has been a steadfast supporter of mental health awareness in athletics, de-stigmatizing conversations about mental wellness by sharing his personal experiences with stress and anxiety. Murray's candor and sincerity have struck a chord with both sports fans and athletes, leading to significant discussions about the demands of top competition and the need to place mental and emotional health first.

A chronic hip issue that threatened to terminate Murray's career early in 2017 was one of the biggest obstacles to his career. Murray refused to allow hardship to define him, even after suffering through many operations and a taxing recuperation process. His incredible return to competitive tennis in 2019 won him the respect and admiration of both colleagues and fans for his fortitude and will to overcome obstacles.

Murray has seen triumphant moments, resiliency, and an unyielding dedication to his profession throughout his career. Murray's impact extends beyond his accomplishments on the tennis court, from his early years as a gifted kid in Dunblane to his rise to the top of the sport. In addition to making a lasting impression on the sport, he has motivated numerous others all around the world to follow their aspirations with fervor, tenacity, and unyielding resolve.

His ascent to fame is evidence of the strength of resiliency, willpower, and an unwavering pursuit of perfection. His path has been characterized by victories, difficulties, and life-changing events that have occurred on and off the tennis court. Murray has a long legacy in the annals of tennis history as a champion, advocate, and role model who inspires and uplifts people of all generations.

CHAPTER 5: FIRST GRAND SLAM SUCCESS

Despite being regarded as one of the most gifted tennis players of his time, Andy Murray battled for many years to win a Grand Slam title—the greatest honor in the game. He almost made it to the finals of the US Open, Wimbledon, and Australian Open many times, but each time he was unsuccessful. His first Grand Slam victory, which ended Britain's 76-year drought for a male Grand Slam singles winner and marked a turning point in Murray's career, occurred at the 2012 US Open. It was a historic event for both British tennis and Murray.

Before the 2012 US Open, Murray had gone through a range of emotions. Heartbreak greeted him in his previous Grand Slam final, and the British public and media put tremendous pressure on him to win a major championship. Murray had grown and persevered despite the high expectations, especially after taking home the gold in the men's singles competition at the London 2012 Olympics.

After this triumph on the revered Wimbledon grass courts, he appeared to have more faith and confidence in his ability.

Murray was seeded third in the 2012 US Open, behind the strong combination of Novak Djokovic and Roger Federer. Murray breezed through the first few rounds, displaying his signature combination of attacking inventiveness and defensive strength. He had to overcome formidable opponents who tested him to the brink of his abilities to make it to the final. But every match seemed to strengthen his determination, and by the time Murray advanced to the semifinals, it was obvious that he was performing at the highest level of his career.

Murray played the formidable opponent Tomas Berdych in the semifinals, who was renowned for his huge serve and groundstrokes. The fierce gusts added a level of hardship to the already challenging conflict. Murray won in four sets, showcasing not just his talent but also his resilience and ability to adjust to challenging circumstances. This triumph prepared the audience for a historic championship match against one of Murray's most formidable opponents, Novak Djokovic.

It was a windy evening in New York for the final, when the wind was again a major factor. It was obvious from away that this would be an incredible combination. In an exhausting opening set that lasted around ninety minutes and ended in a tiebreak, Murray and Djokovic exchanged punches. After a fierce struggle, Murray defeated Djokovic in the tiebreak to win the set 7–6. Murray maintained his winning streak in the second set, breaking Djokovic's serve to win 7–5. Murray was inching closer to his first Grand Slam victory with a two-set lead.

But Djokovic, who is renowned for his extraordinary fortitude and tenacity, made a stunning return. He leveled the match and forced a deciding fifth set by winning the third set 6-2 and the fourth set 6-3. By now, the match was one of the longest US Open finals ever, and it was clear that both players were suffering psychologically and physically. Seeing that he would suffer yet another devastating loss, Murray, who had been here before, mustered all of his willpower and resolve.

Murray discovered an additional gear in the fifth set. With arguably the most forceful and accurate tennis of his career, he broke Djokovic's serve early and maintained his advantage. Sensing the moment's historic significance, the Arthur Ashe Stadium audience sent forth a thunderous cheer in solidarity. Murray remained focused and under tremendous pressure, his serve held strong. As the matches went on, it was evident that Murray was determined to win this time around.

Murray took the court to serve for the title when the fifth set score was 5-2. Despite the obvious strain, Murray stayed calm. Following several tense games, he ultimately put the match away with a powerful serve that Djokovic was unable to return. Murray felt the wave of realization that came with his accomplishment and fell to the ground in shock and delight. It was done; he'd captured his first Grand Slam championship.

For Murray, the win marked a turning point in his career. It was recognition for all the sacrifices, tenacity, and years of hard work he had put into his profession. In addition, it was a source of great pride for British tennis, ending a lengthy run of defeats and motivating a fresh crop of players. Not only was Murray's victory at the 2012 US Open a personal accomplishment, but it was also a victory for everyone who had encouraged and believed in him along the way.

Following his triumph, Murray expressed his sincere thanks to his supporters, family, and team. He recognized the importance of his coach, Ivan Lendl, whose guidance had been crucial in assisting Murray in forging the mental fortitude required to succeed at the greatest level. Murray's career took a turn for the better after his US Open victory, as he went on to win more Grand Slam championships and establish himself as one of the best players of his time.

Andy Murray's maiden Grand Slam victory was evidence of his resilient nature and unwavering willpower. It was a moment that will live on in the annals of tennis history as a representation of overcoming adversity and realizing a lifetime ambition.

For Andy Murray, winning the 2012 US Open was more than just one victory; it was the pinnacle of a lifetime filled with tenacity, development, and unshakable commitment. The enormity of his success started to dawn on him in the days that followed. For Murray, the triumph meant more than just raising the trophy; it meant conquering the obstacles—both physical and mental—that had been in his way for so long.

In the realm of professional tennis, a player's ability and diligence are most fully validated when they win a Grand Slam. The dominating trio of Rafael Nadal, Novak Djokovic, and Roger Federer had won the most Grand Slam championships between them in the years before Murray's breakout, therefore Murray was frequently overlooked by them. Murray experienced intense pressure and scrutiny every time he was on the verge of victory, with many doubting his ability to persevere. His US Open victory put an end to such questions and proved he was a legitimate winner.

The most impressive thing about Murray's win was how flexible and advanced his style of play was. Murray, who was well-known for his counterpunching and defensive abilities, was frequently chastised for being overly submissive in pivotal situations. Murray changed his strategy with the help of Ivan Lendl, a previous Grand Slam winner himself. He started to play with greater aggression, especially when it came to his serve and forehand, which helped him control the game and put his opponents on the defensive. This renewed aggressiveness was evident in the US Open final, where Murray's ability to grab the lead was a key factor in his victory.

The mental component of Murray's game changed significantly as well. Lendl, who had gone through his fair share of Grand Slam disappointments before finally finding success, gave some priceless advice on handling pressure and staying focused. Murray's road to his maiden Grand Slam victory required both mental toughness and physical skill. Murray's willpower was put to the test in the exhausting five-set final against Djokovic, but he remained calm and found the inner strength to get through the worst moments.

Around the world, his achievement struck a deep chord with supporters and aspiring athletes. His narrative exemplified tenacity and fortitude, demonstrating that obstacles and disappointments are inevitable on the path to achievement. Murray's victory ended a lengthy drought for British tennis that had endured since Fred Perry's victory in 1936. The British people, who had been keenly interested in Murray's career, were ecstatic with the win and felt tremendous pride. It was a moment that brought the country together in celebration of an incredible accomplishment.

Following his triumph at the US Open, Murray also received praise and honors from several sources. His position as a national hero was cemented when he was bestowed with other honors, such as the

BBC Sports Personality of the Year. The triumph had a beneficial effect on British tennis as well, encouraging a new generation of players to set lofty objectives and strive toward them. Murray's accomplishment demonstrated that, even in the face of fierce competition, excellence could be attained with perseverance, commitment, and the correct support network.

The self-assurance and conviction Murray had from winning his first Grand Slam championship helped him achieve further success as his career progressed. He became the first British guy to win Wimbledon since 1936 in 2013, fulfilling a lifetime goal. Another memorable and momentous occasion that cemented Murray's legacy in the game was the triumph at Wimbledon. He did not, however, have an easy road. Due to injuries and the intense competition at the highest level of tennis, Murray had to continuously adjust and challenge himself to stay among the best.

When considering his professional life, Murray frequently stressed the value of resiliency and the capacity to overcome obstacles. This tenacity was exemplified by his first Grand Slam victory at the US Open. Every setback, uncertainty, and critique simply strengthened his will to do better and be successful. The triumph served as evidence for the notion that overcoming hardship and always aiming for perfection are the cornerstones of genuine success.

Murray's narrative also emphasized the significance of his support system. Every member of Murray's team, from his coaches and fitness trainers to his family, especially his mother Judy Murray, who was crucial to his early growth, was an important part of his journey. Murray had the support and stability he needed to deal with the ups and downs of playing professional tennis from his close-knit squad. In particular, his collaboration with Ivan Lendl changed everything by providing Murray with a fresh viewpoint and strategy that allowed him to realize his full potential.

Beyond its immediate effects on his career, Andy Murray's maiden Grand Slam victory has left a lasting legacy. It motivates players in various sports by showing that hard work and devotion may result in the achievement of even the most ambitious goals. Murray's triumph serves as a reminder that genuine winners are characterized by their capacity to overcome obstacles and never give up on their dreams of greatness. The road to success is rarely an easy one.

Murray will always have a particular place in his heart for the 2012 US Open when he reflects on his career. It was the point at which years of perseverance, sacrifice, and hard work paid off with the greatest reward. That was the turning point in his career that not only made him a great tennis player but also demonstrated his unwavering determination and drive to succeed. The triumph was a time of shared pride and celebration for the supporters, making it a happy and memorable occasion. It was an important turning point in the history of tennis as it signaled the ascent of a new champion who would go on to have a lasting impact on the game.

CHAPTER 6: OLYMPIC GLORY

Andy Murray's path to Olympic triumph is evidence of his remarkable talent and unwavering devotion. Few could have foreseen the impact he would have as he took the Olympic stage for the first time. Murray, representing Great Britain, went into the Olympics with the same energy and determination that had propelled his career in the business. He saw the Games as a chance to further the sports heritage of his country in addition to achieving personal accomplishment.

For Murray, the London Olympics of 2012 held special significance. The British public held a great deal of expectation and optimism for the event, which was held in his home nation. Only a few weeks prior, Murray had suffered a devastating defeat at the hands of Roger Federer in the Wimbledon final; yet, he returned to the All England Club with a newfound determination. He had a second shot at atonement in the Olympic tennis match, and he took it.

Murray showed a level of energy and talent that astounded both opponents and onlookers throughout the competition. His route to the championship match was paved with clear wins that highlighted his formidable baseline game, accurate serving, and unmatched defensive abilities. Murray's confidence increased with each match, and by the time he got to the championship match, he was playing arguably his greatest tennis ever.

Murray matched up with Federer in the championship match—the same man who had kept him from winning Wimbledon. But this time, the result was different. Encouraged by a fervent home crowd, Murray controlled the game from the off. His aggressive style of play combined with his tactical acumen left Federer perplexed. Murray won in straight sets, earning the gold medal and pulling off a historic success for both Great Britain and himself. His joyful tears running down his cheeks when he was wrapped in the Union Jack became a famous image in Olympic history.

Murray's triumph in London was more than simply a gold medal; it was a turning point that cemented his place among the greatest in the history of the sport. His career was transformed by the victory, which gave him a renewed sense of confidence and fortitude. His gold medal from the Olympics served as a testament to his diligence, fortitude, and capacity to triumph against hardship on the biggest platform.

Murray came back to defend his championship at the Rio de Janeiro Olympics in 2016—four years later. The task was different this time. There was a lot of competition and unexpected settings in Rio. Murray addressed the competition with the same attention and commitment that characterized his last Olympic effort, despite these obstacles.

Murray proved once more in Rio how remarkably capable he is of rising to the moment. His trip to the final was an exhausting test of ability and stamina. He played against several formidable opponents, each of whom tested his mettle. Murray's tenacity, though, came through. He was able to maneuver through the draw because of his strategic savvy and ability to remain composed under duress.

A long duel versus Argentinean star Juan Martin del Potro—known for his strong game and unwavering spirit—was played in the Rio final. The players engaged the fans with their outstanding tennis, making the match an exciting duel. They fought each other for more than four hours, each showing their unrelenting commitment. Ultimately, Murray's unwavering perseverance and exceptional physical preparation proved to be the difference, as he won his second consecutive Olympic gold medal.

at men's singles tennis, winning gold medals at the Olympics back-to-back was an unparalleled feat. Murray's victory in Rio cemented his reputation as one of the best athletes of his age. It was evidence of his dependability, flexibility, and unwavering will to perform at the greatest level.

Murray's Olympic achievement had an effect that went beyond the medals. Young athletes throughout the world, including in Great Britain, were inspired by it. Many people were moved by his journey from a little child with a goal to a double Olympic champion. It emphasized the value of commitment, diligence, and the conviction that everything is attainable with the correct attitude.

His career was also significantly impacted by his Olympic success. His triumphs in Rio and London gave him more confidence, which helped him achieve more on the ATP Tour. He continued to dominate the sport, win additional Grand Slam championships, and regain the top spot in the rankings.

The path to Olympic success was not without difficulties, though. Murray experienced several setbacks, such as injuries and times of self-doubt. But every setback seemed to make him more determined. His capacity to overcome hardship turned into one of his most distinctive qualities. This tenacity won him over supporters and added significance to his achievements.

Andy Murray's Olympic accomplishments stand out as noteworthy turning points in his career. They perfectly capture the spirit of his journey, which was characterized by tenacity, resolve, and an enduring love for the game. His Olympic accomplishments are among the best in tennis history, and they serve as a magnificent example of what can be accomplished with perseverance and hard effort.

His Olympic success is one of his most inspirational moments. It serves as a reminder that real greatness is about more than simply taking home medals; it's also about the experience, the setbacks, and the victories along the route. Andy Murray's Olympic triumph serves as a tribute to the strength of tenacity and the unwavering character of a real victor.

The captivating story of his road to Olympic triumph has captured the attention of both tennis fans and sports aficionados. His Olympic achievements in 2012 and 2016 were not just displays of physical brilliance but also character development, resiliency, and patriotism.

Following the thrill of winning the gold medal at the 2012 London Olympics, Murray's career entered a new phase. Although he was always a strong player, this win made him much more so. He had a psychological advantage from his Wimbledon victory, even if it was for Olympic gold rather than the conventional Grand Slam crown. It demonstrated his ability to triumph over the most formidable opponents on the biggest platforms. His ensuing triumphs and ultimate rise to the top of the global rankings were greatly aided by this newly discovered confidence.

Following the London Olympics, Murray accomplished several noteworthy firsts. He won his maiden Wimbledon championship in 2013, making history as the first British guy to win the competition in 77 years. There was a tangible emotional weight to this accomplishment. For Murray, it represented the achievement of years of perseverance, sacrifice, and facing uncertainties.

One of the most memorable scenes in tennis history is the picture of him crumbling on the sacred grass of Centre Court, overcome with emotion.

Murray's trip was everything but easy, though. Professional tennis demands were taxing on both the body and the mind. A recurring topic that threatened to ruin his career was injuries. Despite these obstacles, Murray remained unwaveringly determined. His capacity to endure suffering and misfortune turned into a distinguishing feature of his professional life.

The 2016 Rio Olympics were preceded by several formidable obstacles. Murray has to battle with persistent hip problems following back surgery in 2013. His endurance and dedication to the sport were put to the test by these physical obstacles. Murray, though, seemed unfazed. He trained extremely hard for Rio, emphasizing both mental toughness and physical fitness. He was aware that he would need to be at the peak of his physical and mental abilities to defend his Olympic championship.

Murray proved in Rio that he could perform well under duress. The enormous stakes and demanding schedule of the Olympic tennis event make it special. As opposed to the Grand Slams, which take place over two weeks, the Olympic competitions are played back-to-back and require maximum effort in each match. Murray handled this difficult situation with his usual tenacity and resolve.

His endurance and adaptability were demonstrated during his run to the championship. He had to contend with a slew of formidable foes, each offering a different challenge. With the likes of Fabio Fognini and the hard-hitting Kei Nishikori, Murray had to constantly modify his style of play and approach. It speaks everything about his great tactical sense and thorough knowledge of the game that he can execute this move with such accuracy.

It was a duel of a lifetime versus Juan Martin del Potro in the final. Del Potro was a tough opponent, having overcome ailments that had threatened his career. The fight was a titanic encounter with protracted rallies, strong blows, and surprising turns. Murray and Del Potro tested each other's physical and mental limitations for more than four hours. Murray's endurance and commitment were put to the test by the searing heat and the exhausting rallies. Nonetheless, Murray's perseverance and experience were evident in those pivotal times. It was amazing how he managed to remain calm and concentrated even when it looked like the match was going away. He was relieved and happy when he eventually prevailed. In addition to successfully defending his Olympic championship, Murray became the first player in tennis history to win two gold medals at the Olympics.

Murray's legacy was significantly impacted by his Olympic accomplishments. They emphasized his reputation as one of the greatest athletes of all time and his exceptional capacity to perform on the largest platforms. His triumphs at the Olympics served as evidence of his tenacity, fortitude, and persistent commitment to his art. They also demonstrated his capacity for motivation and setting an example. Murray's transformation from a gifted juvenile to a two-time Olympic champion serves as an inspiring example of what is possible for those who put in the necessary effort, never give up, and have faith in themselves.

In addition to his accomplishments, Murray's Olympic success had wider societal implications. His triumphs gave his countrymen pride and happiness, as they had long anticipated such tennis moments. They also inspired a new generation of players and spectators and helped the sport become more and more popular in Great Britain.

His Olympic journey is likewise one of metamorphosis. Representing one's nation on a stage of this caliber may come with a lot of pressure. Murray accepted this duty, nevertheless, and used it as inspiration to improve. His Olympic feats were marked by a combination of talent, cunning, and pure willpower. Murray's style was a lesson in intellect and variety, whether it was through his skillful usage of drop drops and volleys, his formidable baseline strokes, or his outstanding defensive play.

His sportsmanship and humility served as a hallmark of his Olympic experience. He always carried himself with grace and respect for his opponents, even in the face of fierce rivalry. His relationships with players, supporters, and the media demonstrated his abiding love of tennis and his function as its representative.

Murray faced further difficulties in the years that followed his second Olympic gold, mostly related to his hip. He subsequently had hip resurfacing surgery, a treatment that many believed would terminate his career, due to the agony and physical restrictions. But Murray, being Murray, would not give up. After undergoing such a major operation, his return to professional tennis was nothing short of amazing. Even when the outcomes weren't all that great, his sheer presence on the court demonstrated his unwavering passion and zest for the game.

His Olympic success is a tale of overcoming adversity and a winner who never lost faith in himself. This narrative speaks to everyone who has overcome obstacles and dared to pursue their dreams. As an Olympic winner, Murray leaves behind more than simply his medals and victories—true greatness is defined by a person's journey, tenacity, and unwavering spirit. His Olympic accomplishments will always be regarded as some of the most amazing and inspirational events in sports history.

CHAPTER 7: INJURIES AND COMEBACKS

Although Andy Murray's career has seen many amazing highs, it has also been marred by serious setbacks that have put his fortitude and will to the test. His tale of setbacks and recoveries is evidence of his steadfast character and commitment to the game of tennis.

Murray has experienced many physical setbacks throughout his career. In 2017, he began to have acute hip pain, which marked the beginning of one of the most difficult seasons. Due to this ailment, which had a major effect on his court play and mobility, he had to withdraw from certain events and leave others early. He was compelled to take a long sabbatical from tennis due to the excruciating discomfort, which was a tough choice for a player who had attained the highest level in the sport.

In January 2018, Murray had hip surgery to get well and resume competitive play. The goal of the surgery was to fix the harm and allow him to return to his former shape. The path to rehabilitation was anything from simple, though. The recovery process was laborious and included rigorous physical therapy and instruction. Murray made an attempt to go back to his prior level of play, but he was unable to do so and questions started to arise about whether he would ever be able to compete at the top level.

Ahead of the 2019 Australian Open, Murray disclosed the depth of his difficulties in a moving news conference. He fought back tears and said that the constant discomfort in his hip may make this his last tournament. The tennis world was rocked by this statement since it appeared like one of the best fighters in history was about to retire. But the Australian Open offered a taste of Murray's unbreakable character. He played a five-set thriller against Roberto Bautista Agut despite the injury, showcasing his characteristic tenacity and willpower. Even though he didn't win the match, his performance served as a testament to his amazing fortitude.

In an attempt to address his persistent pain, Murray decided to have hip resurfacing surgery following the Australian Open, a choice that would change his life. During this procedure, a metal cup that matched the femoral head was implanted in the hip socket. The surgery was a desperate attempt to salvage his job and, more significantly, to raise his standard of living. Despite the difficult recuperation process, Murray never wavered in his resolve. Using social media, he kept his supporters updated on his journey, revealing both the highs and lows of his recovery. The tennis community anxiously awaited his comeback, uncertain about his chances of ever being able to play competitively again.

Five months following his operation, in June 2019, Murray had an incredible recovery. He went back to the court in the Queen's Club Championships when he teamed up with Feliciano Lopez in the doubles division. The two went on to win the event against all odds, with Murray showing glimmers of his previous greatness. This triumph was a crucial turning point in his recuperation as it gave him the self-assurance and conviction that he could still compete at a high level.

Murray kept up this pace and progressively made a comeback to singles tennis. He accomplished yet another incredible accomplishment in October 2019 when he won his first singles championship following hip surgery at the European Open in Antwerp. This win represented his victorious comeback from the verge of retirement and was a significant turning point in his career. Many found encouragement in his path from unbearable suffering to once again holding a trophy, which demonstrated his unwavering perseverance and passion for the sport.

Even after his triumphant return, Murray still faced several obstacles. The strenuous physical requirement of playing professional tennis was wearing his body down. He experienced difficulties, such as further injuries that necessitated his withdrawal from competitions and rearranging his itinerary. Nevertheless, Murray overcame hardships with the same determination that had characterized his professional life. His career was extended by his ability to modify his approach and control his physical state.

Murray's tale demonstrates not just his physical healing but also his mental toughness. It took tremendous mental fortitude to bear the psychological toll of living with chronic pain and the uncertainty of his future. Murray developed techniques for controlling his illness and keeping an optimistic outlook in close collaboration with his team, which included his coach and support personnel. His triumphant comeback to the circuit was largely attributed to his capacity to maintain motivation and concentrate in the face of obstacles.

Murray's presence on the court grew to represent tenacity as he competed. He was still a tough opponent, outmaneuvering competitors who were younger and more physically fit because of his experience and tactical savvy. His signature defensive abilities, astute shot placement, and smart playmaking defined his matches. His mental tenacity and competitive spirit allowed him to be a danger in every match, even when he was not at his physical best.

Murray's path through setbacks and recovery has influenced the sport more broadly as well. His willingness to share his experiences and his candor about his issues have contributed to a greater understanding of the psychological and physical difficulties that sportsmen confront. He is now a proponent of injury avoidance and recuperation, stressing the value of appropriate medical attention and assistance for athletes competing at all levels. Numerous others, both inside and beyond the tennis world, have been motivated to persevere in the face of hardship and tenaciously pursue their ambitions through his narrative.

His incredible ability to recover from injuries and mount victorious comebacks has defined his career. His story serves as a tribute to his remarkable fortitude, unshakable will, and abiding passion for tennis. Murray has accomplished his goals and created a long-lasting legacy of encouragement and tenacity via his hardships and triumphs.

Andy Murray's career has been filled with ups and downs, marked by his exceptional skill on the tennis court and his unwavering fight against injury. His ability to bounce back from these physical setbacks and his incredible comebacks are evidence of his fortitude, tenacity, and passion for tennis.

Murray showed great promise at the beginning of his career. His strong groundstrokes, quick reflexes, and tactical awareness made him a very dangerous opponent. He rose fast through the professional tennis ranks, grabbing the interest of both commentators and spectators. But as his career developed, his body started to suffer from the physical demands of the sport. The first big obstacle was a wrist injury he sustained in 2007 that kept him out of many competitions. Murray persisted in pushing himself despite this setback, exhibiting a degree of tenacity that would come to define his career.

But it was his hip that was the most serious and enduring issue Murray had during his career. His right hip started to hurt badly in 2017, which had a major impact on how well he played on the court. Physiotherapy and pain management were used to treat the injuries at first, but as the years went on, it became evident that these approaches were ineffective. As the discomfort worsened, it became more difficult for him to compete at his typically high level since it affected his mobility. The persistent pain limited Murray's once-smooth movement on the court, which caused him to withdraw early from multiple competitions and sparked questions about his long-term prospects in the game.

In January 2018, Murray decided to have hip surgery in an attempt to resolve the problem. The goal of the hip arthroscopy treatment was to fix further joint injuries as well as a rupture in the labrum. Although the operation was a significant milestone, it also marked the start of a protracted and difficult recuperation process. Murray had months of recovery following surgery, which included rigorous physical therapy and training. Regaining the strength and flexibility required to play professional tennis at the top level was the aim in addition to healing.

There were several obstacles in the way of healing. Murray did not have much luck getting back to his former self. His hip problem lingered, and questions about his ability to play at a high level started to arise. The accident had a severe psychological and physical toll, and for a while, it appeared as though his brilliant career may be ending too soon. Murray, who was always renowned for his tenacity and spirit of battle, found this time to be especially trying. It was a great strain to live with the uncertainty of his sports career.

Murray disclosed the breadth of his challenges at a tearful press conference in January 2019, just before the Australian Open. He fought back tears as he said that the hip pain had gotten so bad that this tournament could be his last. The revelation stunned and saddened supporters and teammates, who had grown to respect Murray for his ability as well as his perseverance and sportsmanship. Murray decided to play in the Australian Open despite the agony because he wanted to give it his best one final time. His first-round victory over Roberto Bautista Agut came to represent his unwavering determination. Even though he was ultimately defeated in a taxing five-set match, his performance demonstrated his bravery and tenacity.

Murray took a life-altering choice to have hip resurfacing surgery after the Australian Open. In this more drastic treatment, the hip socket was filled with a metal cup that matched the metal cap that covered the femoral head. Relieving his chronic pain and enabling him to have a better quality of life was the aim. There was no assurance that he would be able to play competitive tennis again, so the surgery carried a big risk. Murray was prepared to accept that risk, though, in the hopes of extending his career and returning to anything like normalcy.

Following hip resurfacing surgery, the healing process was difficult and prolonged. To restore his strength and mobility, Murray had to undergo months of rehabilitation and work nonstop with his medical staff. The physical treatment was taxing and needed endurance and patience. Murray was transparent about his experience at this time, posting updates on social media and giving readers a peek at the highs and lows of his rehabilitation. His openness and honesty won him over admirers and served as motivation for those going through comparable struggles.

Five months after his operation, in June 2019, Murray made a stunning comeback to the court at the Queen's Club Championships. He surprised everyone by winning the championship in the doubles division alongside Feliciano Lopez. This win was a huge turning point since it provided Murray with confidence in addition to its symbolic significance. It demonstrated unequivocally that he was still capable of competing and succeeding at a high level despite the circumstances. Murray's victory at Queen's Club served as a poignant reminder of his tenacity and willpower.

Encouraged by this triumph, Murray progressively returned to singles play. Another noteworthy accomplishment came in October 2019, when he won the European Open in Antwerp. It was especially meaningful for him to win this singles championship after having hip surgery. Murray had faced many obstacles and uncertainties along the way, but his unflinching drive saw him through to the finish line. His victory in Antwerp was evidence of his extraordinary work ethic and mental fortitude. Even with these accomplishments, Murray's path was not without difficulties. The physical demands of playing professional tennis remained difficult. He had further setbacks and injuries, which made it necessary for him to change his schedule and withdraw from competitions. Murray was put to the test by every setback, yet he never gave up. His career was extended by his ability to modify his approach and control his physical state. He collaborated carefully with his group to devise tactics that would maximize his ability to compete while lowering the possibility of more injuries.

His narrative demonstrates not just physical healing but also mental fortitude. It took tremendous mental fortitude to bear the psychological toll of living with chronic pain and the uncertainty of his future. Murray's successful comeback to the tour was largely due to his ability to maintain motivation and focus in the face of adversity. His story has served as an inspiration to many, demonstrating the strength of tenacity and will in the face of difficulty. Murray has become an advocate for injury prevention and recovery as a result of his hardships and achievements. His candor about his difficulties has contributed to a greater understanding of the psychological and physical strain of professional athletics. Using his position to draw attention to the need for improved resources and support systems, he has underlined the need for appropriate medical care and assistance for athletes at all levels. Numerous others, both inside and beyond the tennis world, have been motivated to persist through their hardships and tenaciously pursue their objectives by his narrative.

His incredible ability to recover from injuries and mount victorious comebacks has defined his career. His story serves as a tribute to his remarkable fortitude, unshakable will, and abiding passion for tennis. Murray has accomplished his goals and created a long-lasting legacy of encouragement and tenacity via his hardships and triumphs. His experience serves as a potent reminder that even the most difficult obstacles may be conquered with perseverance and hard effort.

CHAPTER 8: SECOND GRAND SLAM WIN

Andy Murray's career-defining achievement of winning his second Grand Slam match cemented his place among the best players in men's tennis. The victory occurred at the 2013 Wimbledon Championships, a competition with a rich legacy in British sports culture. Murray's difficult and intense route to this title reflected not just his physical skill but also his tenacity and willpower.

Murray has already made a reputation for himself as a competitor in Grand Slam competitions before Wimbledon 2013. He had advanced to several finals, losing to Roger Federer in the Wimbledon final in 2012. His ambition to be successful on the renowned grass courts of the All England Club was further heightened by this close call.

British supporters, who had been waiting for a native winner, had higher hopes going into the 2013 competition. Murray handled the pressure with his trademark poise, moving through the rounds with a combination of unflinching focus and strategic genius. His journey to the final was paved with arduous victories against strong opponents, demonstrating his versatility as a player.

In the eagerly awaited championship match, Murray squared up against the top-seeded and reigning champion, Novak Djokovic. Witnessing a titanic battle, millions of people tuned in to an electrifying environment. Murray had a well-thought-out game strategy that included aggressive shot-making and strong defense to unnerve his opponent.

Both competitors strained one other's physical and mental stamina as the competition developed into a tense, hotly contested encounter. Murray had a steely resolution in high-stress circumstances, demonstrating his fortitude during pivotal occasions. Usually a dependable weapon, his serve provided vital aces and well-timed deliveries to keep Djokovic at bay.

Murray's confidence increased during the match as a result of the enthusiastic Center Court audience's backing. There was thunderous applause after each point he scored, which motivated him to keep going for the gold. Despite many challenges from the tenacious Djokovic, Murray stayed unwavering and refused to give up.

In a thrilling finale, Murray won with a strong serve that Djokovic was unable to return, setting forth a joyful and relieved burst from both Murray and his supporters. Murray's triumphant collapse to the turf, filled with emotion at realizing a longstanding desire on home soil, made the occasion emotional.

Murray's victory at Wimbledon meant more than just individual recognition. It gave British tennis a fresh lease on life, motivating a generation of players and stoking patriotism. Murray's legacy in the sport is evidenced by his devotion to his trade, his tenacity in the face of difficulty, and his unshakable commitment to perfection.

In addition to being a career highlight, his 2013 Wimbledon victory at the second Grand Slam level is evidence of the strength of resiliency and willpower in the face of extreme adversity. Andy Murray has cemented his legacy as a tennis champion by achieving this ultimate moment, which epitomizes the zenith of sports accomplishment.

More than just a triumph on the tennis court, his second Grand Slam win at the 2013 Wimbledon Championships was the result of years of hard work, tenacity, and determination, and it demonstrated his unrelenting commitment to perfection. Murray's story as a world-class athlete has more depth because of the difficulties and emotional highs and lows he experienced along the way to this historic victory.

When Murray arrived at Wimbledon in 2013, he carried a lot of expectations, both national and personal. Though it had left a sour taste, the final defeat to Roger Federer the year before had strengthened his resolve to come back even stronger. Murray stood out during the event thanks to his unique combination of mental toughness and tactical skill. His careful planning, polished abilities, and calculated approach to the game showed in every match that led to the championship.

Murray had his most difficult test yet in the final match against Novak Djokovic. The current world No. 1 and ferocious adversary Djokovic came prepared, testing Murray's mental and physical stamina to the breaking point. With neither player willing to give up an inch, the match turned into a brutal war of attrition. Murray's capacity to stay composed under duress and make accurate strokes was essential against Djokovic's constant counterattacks.

The energy at Centre Court was palpable, as a sea of British flags and passionate fans gathered to support their hometown hero. The famous Wimbledon grounds resounded with deafening cheers at every point that Murray won. As Murray attempted to become the first British man to win the Wimbledon singles championship in 77 years, the weight of history hung heavily in the air.

The intensity of the match increased with each game and rally as it neared its conclusion. Murray faced Djokovic's assault and took on crucial chances, demonstrating his tenacity and mental endurance. Throughout the tournament, his serve proved to be a formidable weapon, producing critical aces and well-placed deliveries that kept Djokovic off balance.

Murray's resolve showed through in the match's pivotal stages. He unleashed a barrage of lightning-fast groundstrokes and accurate volleys that left Djokovic reeling as the audience erupted in cheers. Murray was in the clear after a crucial break of serve and a hold to love. His nerves of steel became evident in the decisive game, as he finished the match with composure and assurance.

The triumphant moment was utterly wonderful. In shock and delight, Murray fell to his knees when Djokovic's comeback missed the mark. As he accepted the enormity of his accomplishment—realizing a longtime ambition on Wimbledon's sacred grass—cries fell down his face. Not only did Murray experience overwhelming emotions, but the whole country did too, as Britain rejoiced over a momentous athletic achievement.

Apart from the individual honors, Murray's second Grand Slam triumph had a significant impact on British tennis. It spurred a comeback in the game, inspiring young athletes all across the nation to take up a racket and pursue their dreams. His accomplishments cleared the path for the next generations, changing the British tennis scene and solidifying his reputation as a pioneer.

His path has been characterized by perseverance in the face of difficulty. He has won many admirers all across the world with his steadfast dedication to his trade and indomitable spirit, despite facing setbacks and injuries. His influence extends beyond tennis with his humanitarian work and support of gender parity in the game.

The 2013 Wimbledon double crown is the pinnacle of sports achievement. It's a tale about tenacity, resolve, and striving for greatness in the face of adversity. His transformation from a gifted young athlete with goals to a multiple Grand Slam winner and gold medallist at the Olympics is proof of the strength of drive and passion. For future generations, his tennis legacy will serve as a source of inspiration and a constant reminder that goals can be accomplished with perseverance, hard effort, and faith.

CHAPTER 9: WORLD NO. 1

Andy Murray's rise to the top of the men's tennis rankings as the World No. 1 is a credit to his tenacity, tenacity, and extraordinary talent on the field. Murray, a Scottish native, showed an early talent for tennis and developed his skills through intense practice and competition. His ascent to the top of the rankings was paved with failures, victories, and an unwavering dedication to perfection.

Years of arduous labor and deliberate growth under the direction of his coaches and mentors culminated in Murray's ascent to the top of the world rankings. In the middle of the 2000s, he made his debut in the top division of professional tennis, displaying his skill with noteworthy triumphs and consistent advancement in important competitions. His mental toughness and ability to adjust his approach during games were hallmarks of his style of play.

Murray faced tough opponents during his career, including Rafael Nadal, Novak Djokovic, and tennis great Roger Federer. In particular, his rivalry with Djokovic elevated both players to unprecedented levels of athleticism and performance, making it one of the highlights of contemporary tennis. Murray gained the respect and affection of both teammates and spectators for his tenacity in these fierce competitions.

A notable accomplishment for Murray was earning the No. 1 spot in the world rankings in November of 2016. This achievement not only confirmed his status as one of the best tennis players of his time but also recognized the years of hard effort he had put in. His rise to the top was evidence of his versatility, consistency, and capacity to perform well in high-stress situations at the toughest venues in the sport.

Murray ranked No. 1, kept up his impressive form, showcasing his command of every facet of the game. His tactical savvy, strong groundstrokes, and clever playmaking enabled him to win matches even against the most formidable opponents. Murray stands himself as a great champion because of his mental toughness and capacity to maintain concentration during pivotal moments in matches, which go beyond his technical prowess.

His influence went beyond his sporting prowess. He gained recognition for his humanitarian work by funding several programs and organizations that encouraged young people to play tennis and increased accessibility to sporting facilities. He received honors and acclaim from the sporting world as well as outside of it for his services to tennis and society.

Murray encountered difficulties during his career, like as injuries that may have stopped him in his tracks. Nonetheless, his tenacity and will to triumph over hardship were crucial to his ongoing success. He demonstrated his unrelenting dedication to his trade and his ongoing enthusiasm for the game through his ability to recover from setbacks and resume his best performance.

His time as the World No. 1 represents all that makes a real champion. His rise from a young, talented player to one of the best athletes in tennis history is a credit to his ability, tenacity, and commitment. Murray's importance in tennis history is furthered by his influence on the game and his legacy as a global role model for aspiring sportsmen.

His tenure as the world's top tennis player is a noteworthy accomplishment in the sport's illustrious past, characterized by a path of tenacity, victories, and pivotal events that molded his reputation. Murray was raised by devoted teachers who saw his natural potential and unwavering perseverance. He was raised in Dunblane, Scotland, and spent his early years surrounded by tennis.

Murray showed early signs of prodigious skill on the court, combining a strong combination of physical prowess and mental toughness with tactical acumen. His ascent through the junior tennis levels portended a remarkable career characterized by an unwavering quest for perfection that would later come to characterize his reign as the dominating force in men's tennis.

There were obstacles in his way of becoming the World No. 1 player. He encountered detractors early in his professional career who doubted his capacity for elite competition. Unfazed, Murray kept honing his craft, improving his abilities in all fields, and creating a strategy that would come to define his style. Significant wins at renowned competitions, such as his first Grand Slam victory at the 2012 US Open, marked his breakthrough and cemented his place among the game's greatest players.

A period of tennis marked by intense competitiveness and unmatched skill was defined by the rivalry between Murray, Roger Federer, Rafael Nadal, and Novak Djokovic. Murray's on-court struggles with his peers went beyond simple sports rivalry, demonstrating his capacity to modify his style to neutralize his opponents' advantages and win crucial matches.

Murray reached the peak of his career in November 2016 when he achieved the World No. 1 ranking.

This accomplishment demonstrated his perseverance, resiliency, and unshakable dedication to constant progress rather than just his ranking points. Murray, the player with the highest ranking, managed the difficulties of holding onto that place while pushing himself to improve even more.

Murray's reign as the world's top player was defined by an exhibition of tennis skills that went beyond quantitative successes. His legacy was defined by his capacity to perform well under duress, carry out tactical game plans, and display mental toughness when things mattered most during games. In addition to his many honors and championships, Murray's influence on tennis surpassed all previous generations of players and spectators globally.

His charitable activities demonstrated his dedication to changing society for the better. He supported several humanitarian projects, including programs that helped impoverished kids have better access to sports and medical research. His efforts off the court reflected his commitment to tennis greatness, exhibiting a comprehensive strategy for using his position for social benefit.

Murray had hardship throughout his career in the form of injuries that put his fortitude and tenacity to the test. His capacity to bounce back from physical setbacks and reach his best performance levels demonstrated his mental fortitude and will to face challenges. Murray's everlasting love for the game and his unrelenting quest to realize his athletic potential was demonstrated by each of his comebacks.

His reign as the world's top player goes beyond what is considered to be the pinnacle of tennis brilliance; he embodies tenacity, fortitude, and a commitment to skill. His rise from a budding tennis player to a global hero is proof of the sport's transformational power and capacity to uplift and bring people together from all walks of life. Fans and aspiring sportsmen continue to be inspired by his career as a champion, both on and off the court, and he has left an enduring impression on the annals of tennis history and sportsmanship.

CHAPTER 10: LATER CAREER AND LEGACY

Andy Murray's perseverance, tenacity, and unshakable dedication to tennis greatness are demonstrated by his later career and legacy. Murray faced tremendous obstacles on and off the court as his career approached its later phases, but his unwavering love for the game and his unwavering drive for achievement remained the hallmarks of his path.

Murray's career took off after he became the first British man to win the Wimbledon singles championship in 77 years in 2013 with his historic triumph. His victories at Wimbledon in 2016 and the US Open in 2012 cemented his place among the greatest tennis players of all time. In addition to his strategic acumen and mental toughness, Murray's versatility on the field made him stand out in the competition.

But there were also major setbacks in Murray's later career, mostly because of nagging ailments, including a hip issue that almost ended his career. Murray was adamant that he would return to competitive tennis even after having many operations and needing to recover for extended periods. His ability to bounce back from hardship won him admirers across the globe and solidified his status as a warrior on and off the court.

Murray's impact goes much beyond his accomplishments and his on-court exploits. He was a major force behind the change in British tennis, encouraging a new wave of players and increasing the game's appeal throughout the United Kingdom. Murray's effect was international because of his sportsmanship and competitive spirit, which won him respect and affection from people all over the world.

His influence went beyond tennis, as seen by his charitable endeavors and support of several organizations. His vocal advocacy for gender parity in athletics and his efforts to increase impoverished children's access to tennis underscored his dedication to social responsibility.

Murray's tenacity and fortitude emerged as distinguishing characteristics of his legacy as he overcame the difficulties of his later career. His place among tennis legends was cemented by his ability to rise above adversity and his undying devotion to his art. Murray's legacy will live on long after he retires thanks to his contributions to tennis and his lasting influence on the next generations of players.

His subsequent career and legacy are the epitome of what it means to be a champion: they are characterized by tenacity, passion, and celebration for his lasting impact on the tennis world and beyond.

During his latter career, he overcame many obstacles and experienced times of difficulty that tried his determination and fortitude. Murray's will to overcome the difficulties of reoccurring injuries and reach his best was truly motivating. He suffered from a hip problem for years, requiring several operations and long durations of rehabilitation. Although many people didn't think Murray would be able to return to his previous level of success, his unwavering attitude and unrelenting work ethic motivated him to try.

Murray's courtside strategic genius and tactical awareness were well known throughout his career. His ability to outsmart opponents and make accurate shots under duress were defining characteristics of his game. Murray's devotion to perfection was demonstrated by his readiness to modify his style of play in order to meet and surpass new obstacles.

His influence went beyond the game of tennis. He always championed equal chances for female athletes by using his platform, and his campaign for gender equality in sports struck a deep chord. Murray's strong advocacy for programs that encourage inclusivity and diversity in tennis demonstrates his dedication to creating a fairer sporting environment.

Murray's impact on British tennis persisted even as he neared the end of his career. He spurred a renewed interest in and involvement in the game, especially among younger players hoping to follow in his footsteps. Murray became a legend in the tennis world and beyond thanks to his accomplishments, which included his historic victories at Wimbledon and the US Open.

In addition to his athletic accomplishments, Murray had a lasting impact via his charitable work. His philanthropic organization funded a wide range of projects, such as programs to increase underprivileged children's access to sports and endeavors to address social concerns via community engagement and education. Murray believed in leveraging his position to effect constructive social change, which was seen by his dedication to giving back.

Murray had failures, but his fortitude and will to triumph despite hardship remained constant. His mental toughness and pure tenacity were on display as he recovered from injury setbacks and continued to compete fiercely against younger opponents. Murray's thrilling comeback wins, which were frequently characterized by dramatic rallies and fierce bouts, enthralled spectators and confirmed his place as a fan favorite.

Murray's status as a tennis hero and inspiration for young sportsmen remained solid as he considered the end of his career. Millions of people worldwide were impressed by his transformation from a young, gifted athlete to a multiple Grand Slam winner and Olympic gold medallist. Murray's influence extended beyond athletics, as he turned into a representation of tenacity, good sportsmanship, and commitment to perfection.

His subsequent work and lasting impact serve as a tribute to the strength of resiliency, willpower, and unrelenting enthusiasm. His perseverance in overcoming hardships on and off the court, as well as his enduring influence on tennis and society at large, guarantee that his legacy will serve as an inspiration to next generations of sportsmen and activists for many years to come. His path serves as a reminder that character and principles upheld throughout one's career are just as important indicators of real greatness as achievements.

CONCLUSION

Andy Murray's career has been characterized by his perseverance, tenacity, and unwavering quest for tennis court greatness. As we get to the close of our examination of his journey, it is clear that Murray's influence goes much beyond his many honors. His achievements as one of the best British tennis players of all time have been solidified by his victories at Wimbledon, the US Open, and the Olympics.

Murray has had several difficulties throughout his career, both on and off the court. Murray has consistently demonstrated a remarkable capacity to recover from setbacks, whether it be from injuries that threatened to end his career or from the extreme strain of playing at the greatest level. Numerous admirers and aspiring sportsmen worldwide have been impressed by his mental tenacity and unshakable dedication to his trade.

Murray has made more contributions to tennis than just his winnings. He has made a strong case for gender parity in tennis by criticizing the differences in opportunities and prize money that female players get. Peers and supporters alike have respected and appreciated him for his advocacy of women's rights in sports.

His charitable endeavors have had a noteworthy influence. His dedication to giving back to the community is evident in the significant sums of money he has generated for several charitable causes through his Andy Murray Live charity exhibition events. Beyond the tennis court, Murray has shaped the sport's future and left a lasting legacy that will be cherished for a very long time.

One thing is evident when we consider Andy Murray's journey: his love of tennis and his will to win have made him stand out as a great champion. His is a narrative of not just athletic success but one of bravery, resiliency, and the unwavering pursuit of excellence. Andy Murray's career has had a lasting impression on the sports world and beyond, inspiring people to pursue their goals and overcome challenges.

His ascent to tennis stardom is evidence of his tenacity and commitment. His career has been characterized by remarkable incidents that have enthralled spectators around and motivated a fresh crop of sportsmen. It's evident when we learn more about Murray's contributions to the game that his legacy goes beyond wins and stats.

The unwavering work ethic and intense competition that drove Murray to the top of the tennis world are the keys to his success. He is regarded as a tactical genius on the court because of his capacity to modify his style and plan strategies for even the most formidable opponents. Murray's development as a player, from perfecting defensive play to honing a potent serve, is a testament to his dedication to innovation and constant progress.

Murray has developed rivalries with some of the best players of his generation throughout the course of his career, including Novak Djokovic, Rafael Nadal, and Roger Federer. These titanic fights have not only demonstrated his talent and tenacity, but they have also raised the bar for excitement and intensity in the sport. Murray's status as a big-match player has been cemented by his capacity to perform well under duress and in pivotal situations.

His influence goes beyond his sporting prowess. After surviving serious injuries and setbacks to regain his ranking among the world's best tennis players, he has come to represent tenacity and fortitude. His openness regarding mental health issues and his support for more understanding and assistance have spurred significant discussions both inside and outside of the sports world.

Murray's charitable deeds have also had a lasting impression on society. He has significantly aided causes ranging from children's education to healthcare and environmental protection through his philanthropic foundation and participation in several community activities. His dedication to give back is more evidence of his conviction that he should use his position to effect good change and leave an enduring legacy off the court.

As we come to the end of our examination of Andy Murray's career, it is impossible not to be amazed by the extent and profundity of his influence on tennis and other sports. His transformation from a gifted young athlete to a well-known sports figure worldwide is proof of the strength of drive, tenacity, and purpose. Future generations of athletes will continue to draw inspiration from Andy Murray's legacy to set lofty goals, put in a lot of effort, and never give up.

Printed in Great Britain
by Amazon